Travel to the ARCTIC

Author and Illustrator Tetiana ElerT

ARCTIC

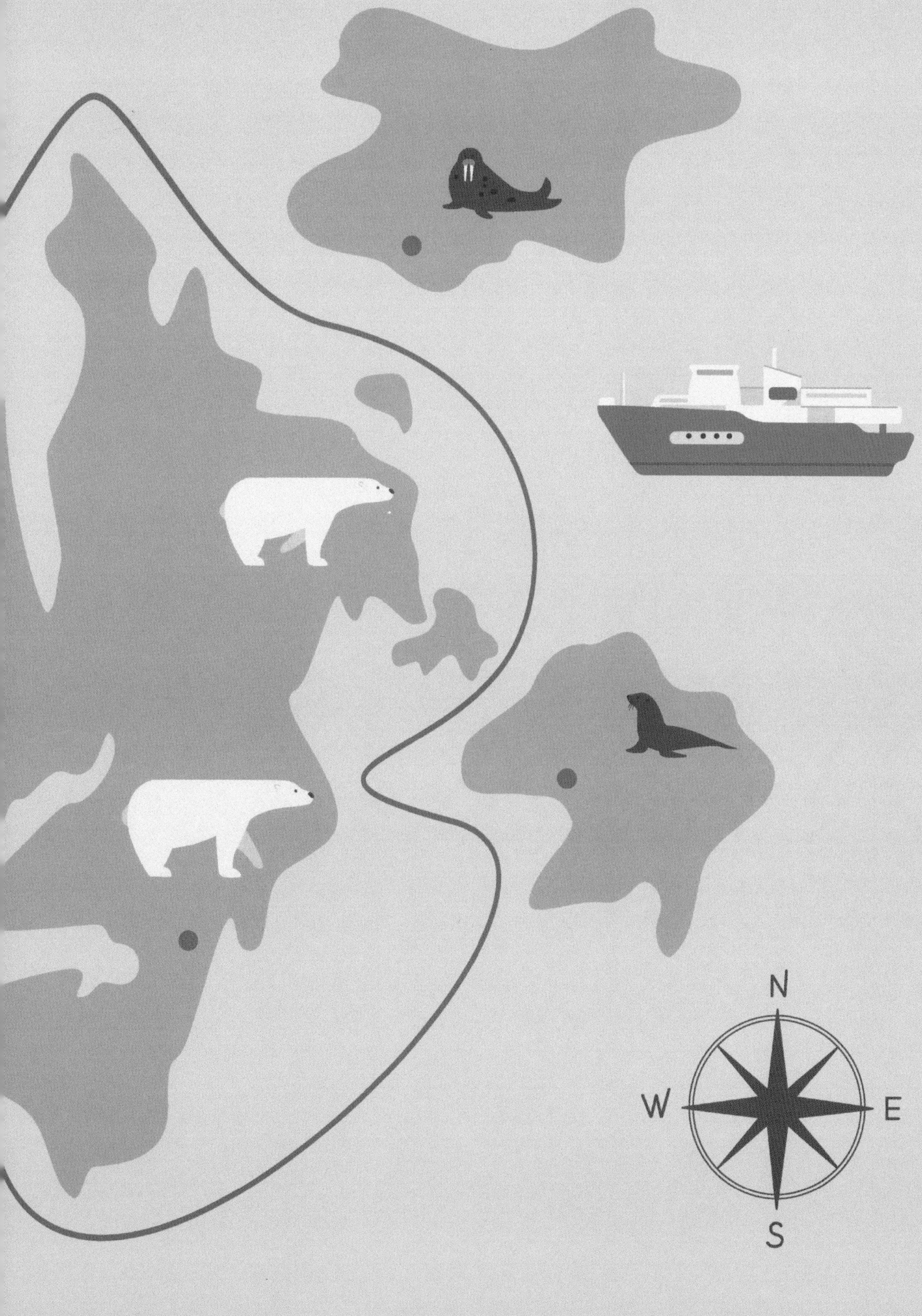
N
W
E
S

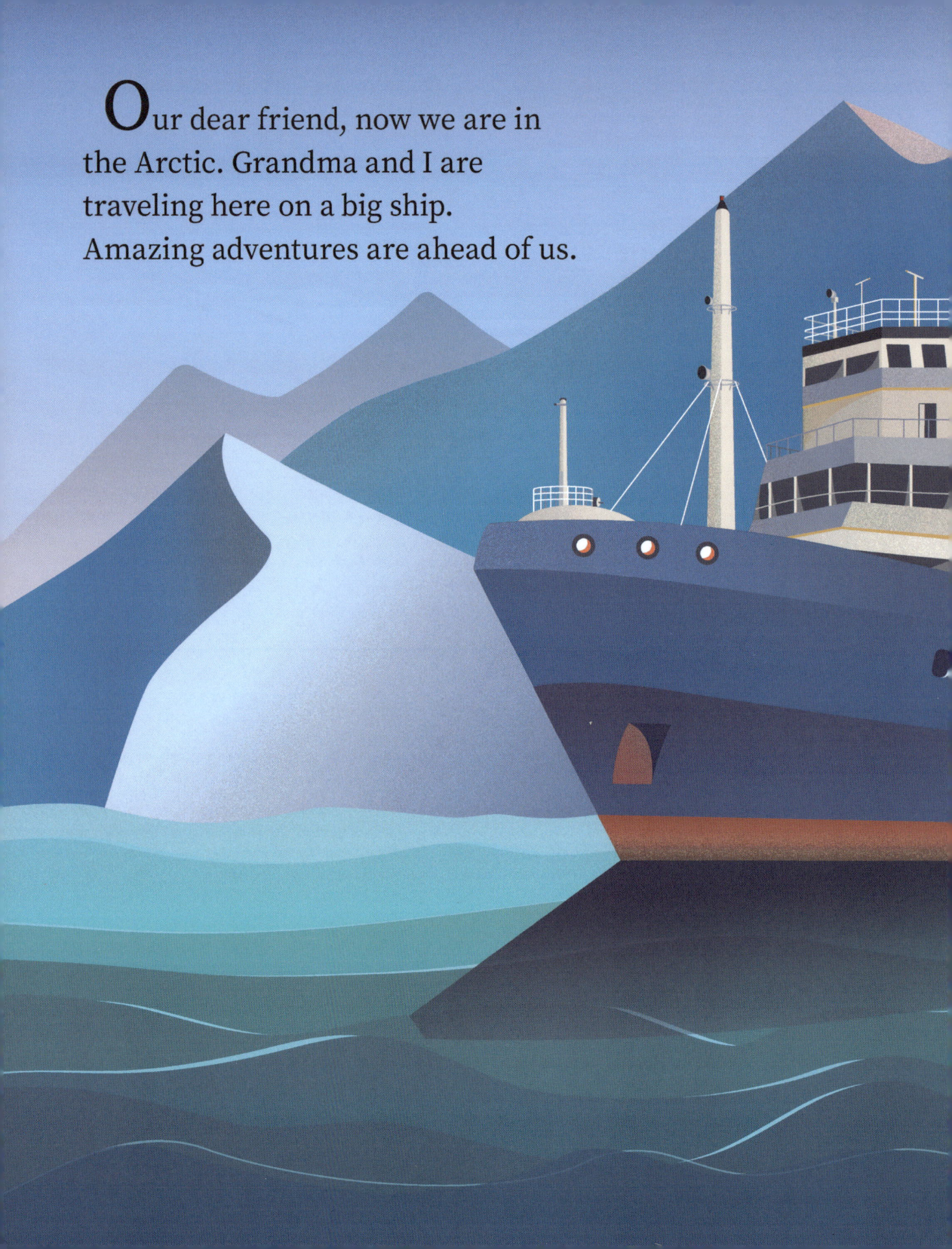

Our dear friend, now we are in the Arctic. Grandma and I are traveling here on a big ship. Amazing adventures are ahead of us.

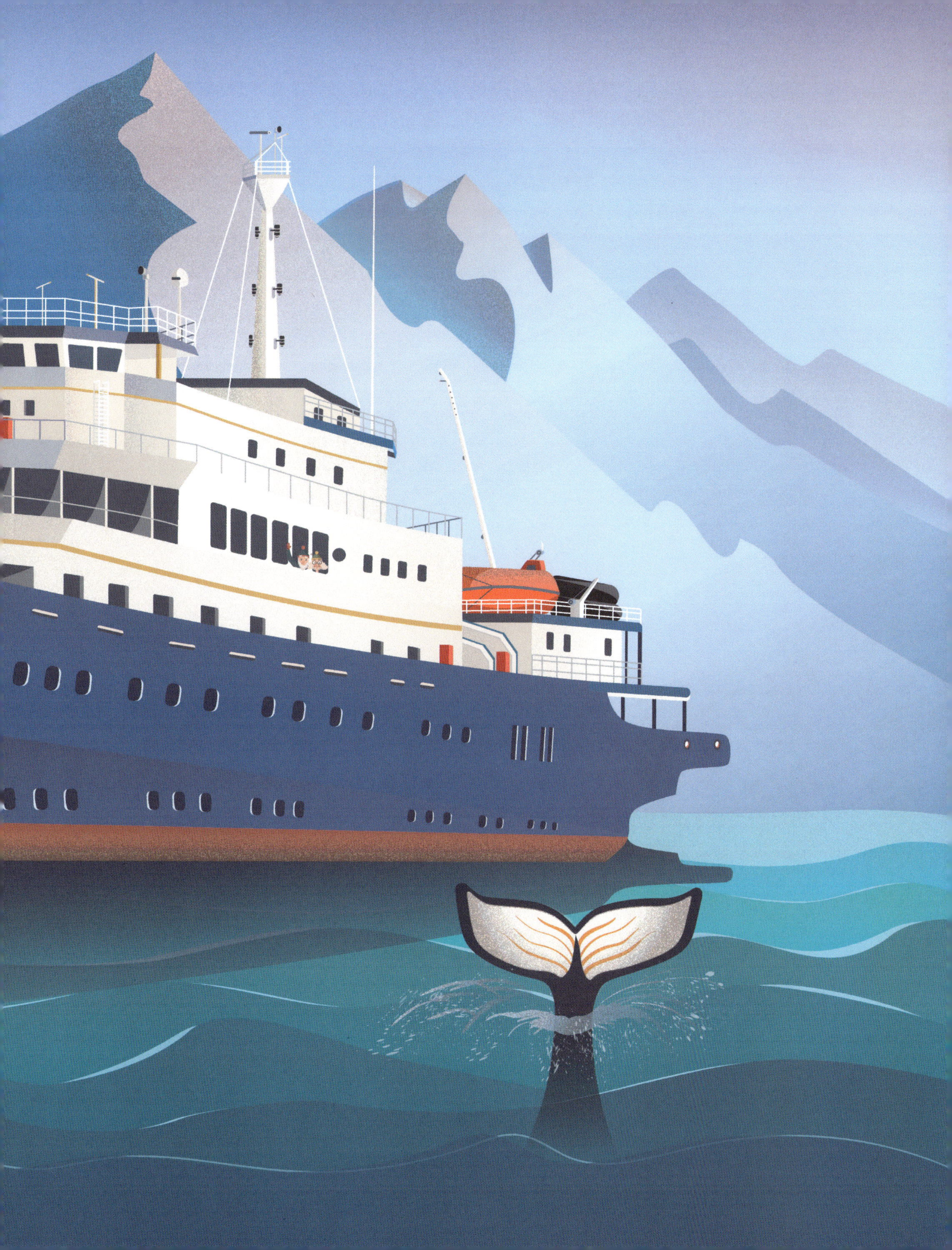

Orca whales spotted us immediately.

They told Mr. Walrus right away that the guests had arrived, and then...

Grandma and I saw a family of Arctic seals on the shore - daddy seal, mommy seal, and a baby seal.

We took a picture together and went on.

Then we were met by a puffin. "Welcome to our land! Unforgettable adventures are waiting for you! Follow this path to that house," said the puffin, fluttering his wings and flying away.

welcome

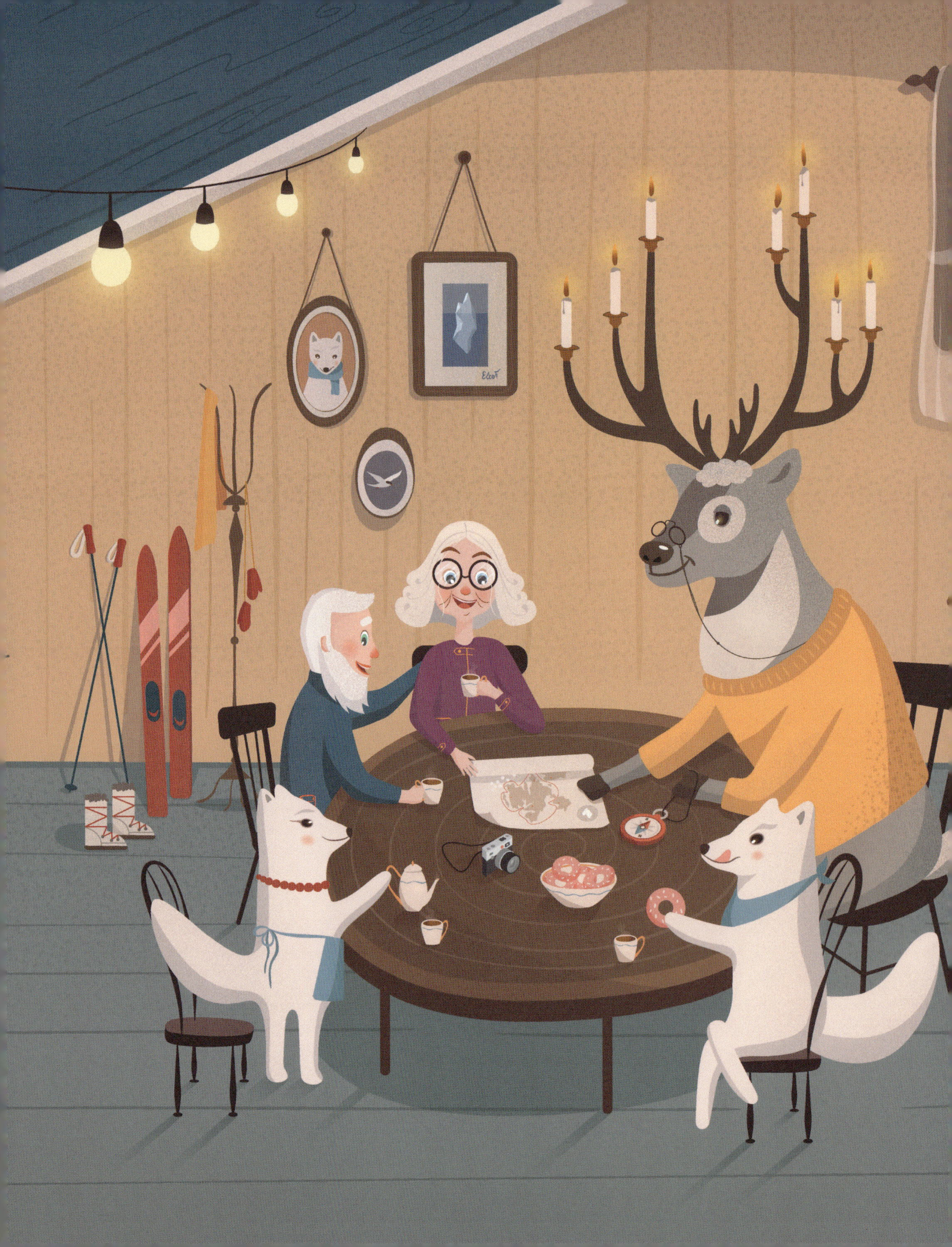

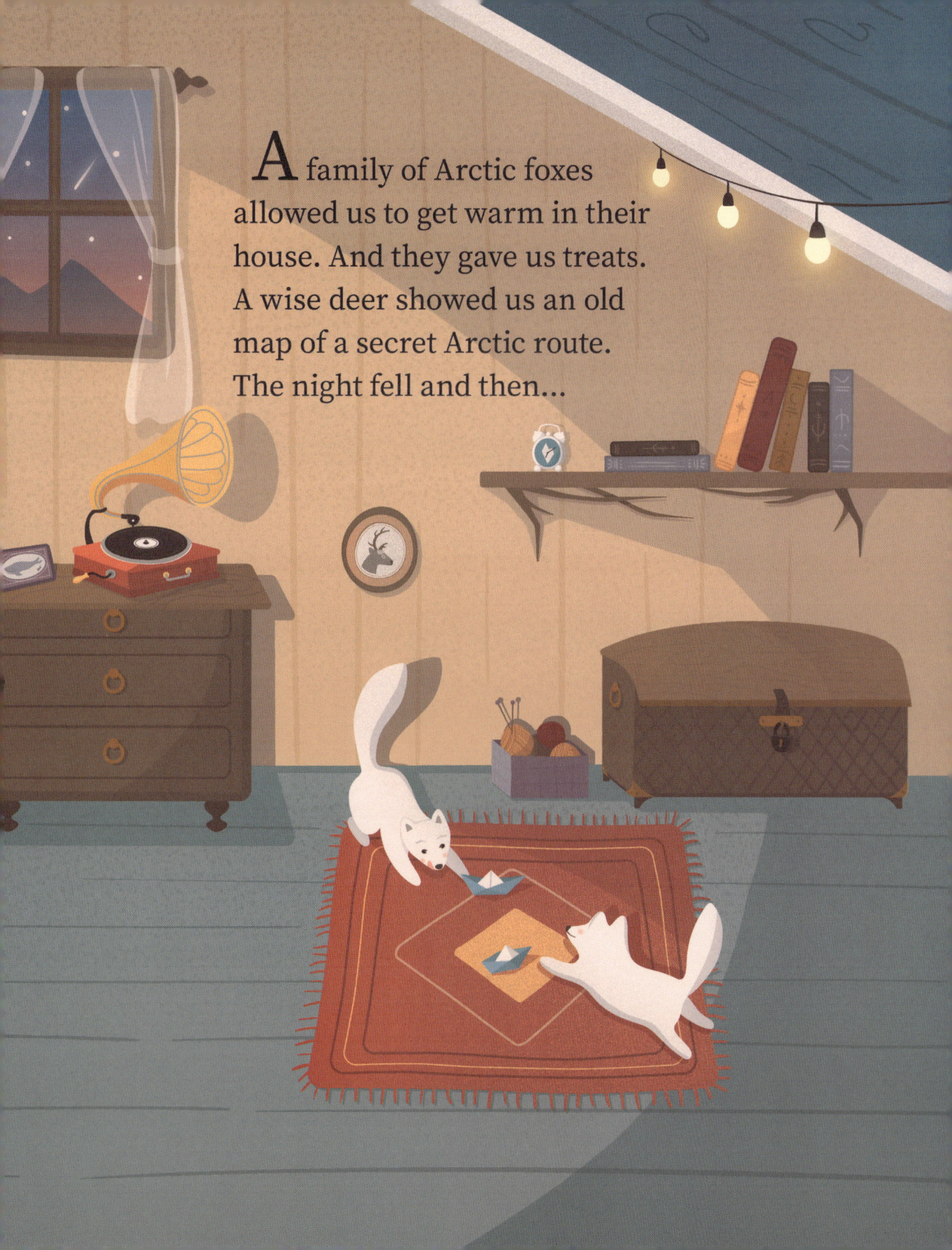

A family of Arctic foxes allowed us to get warm in their house. And they gave us treats. A wise deer showed us an old map of a secret Arctic route. The night fell and then…

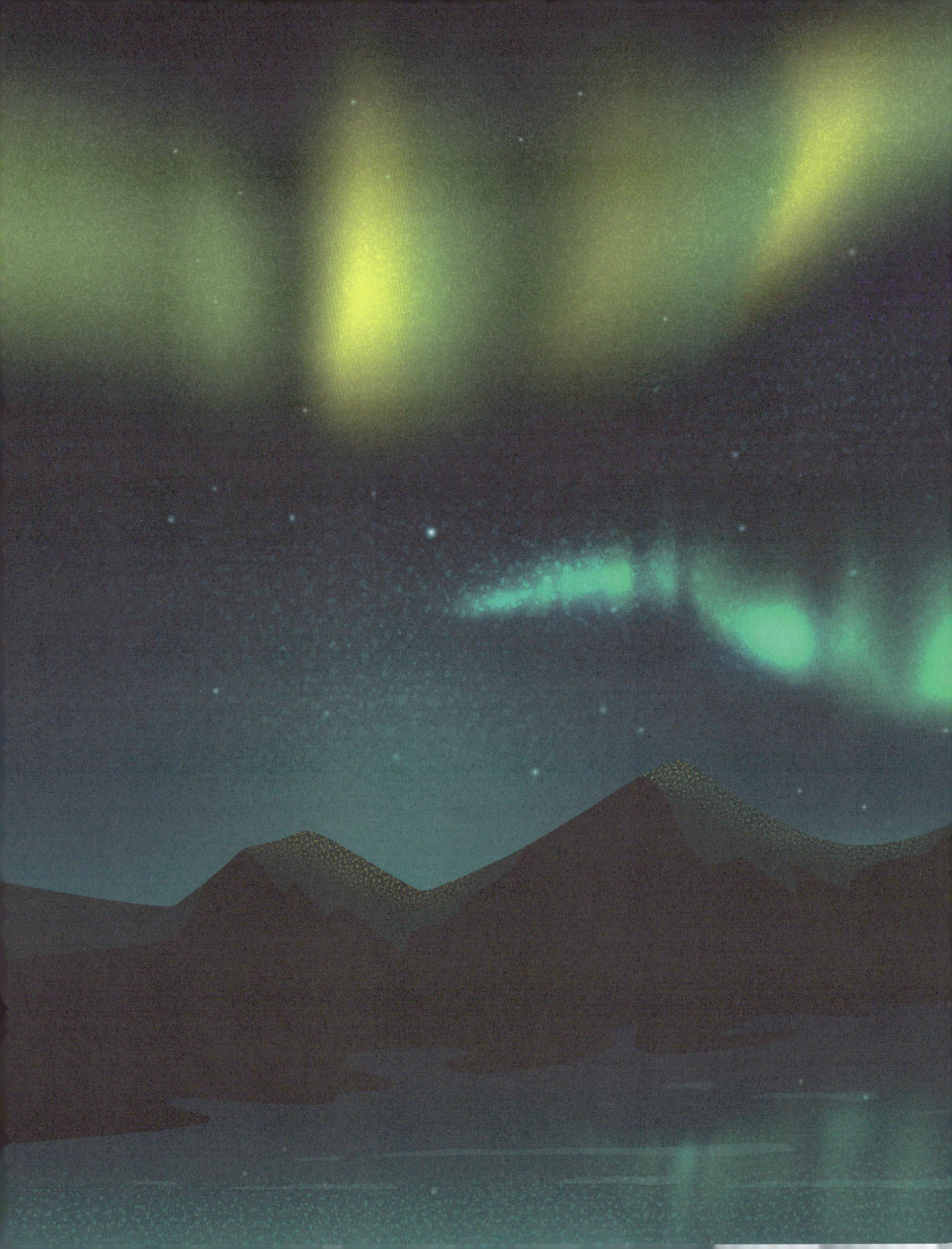

Wow!

We met a fun family of polar bears in the Arctic. Daddy bear, mommy bear, and two baby bears.

Here is what we decided...

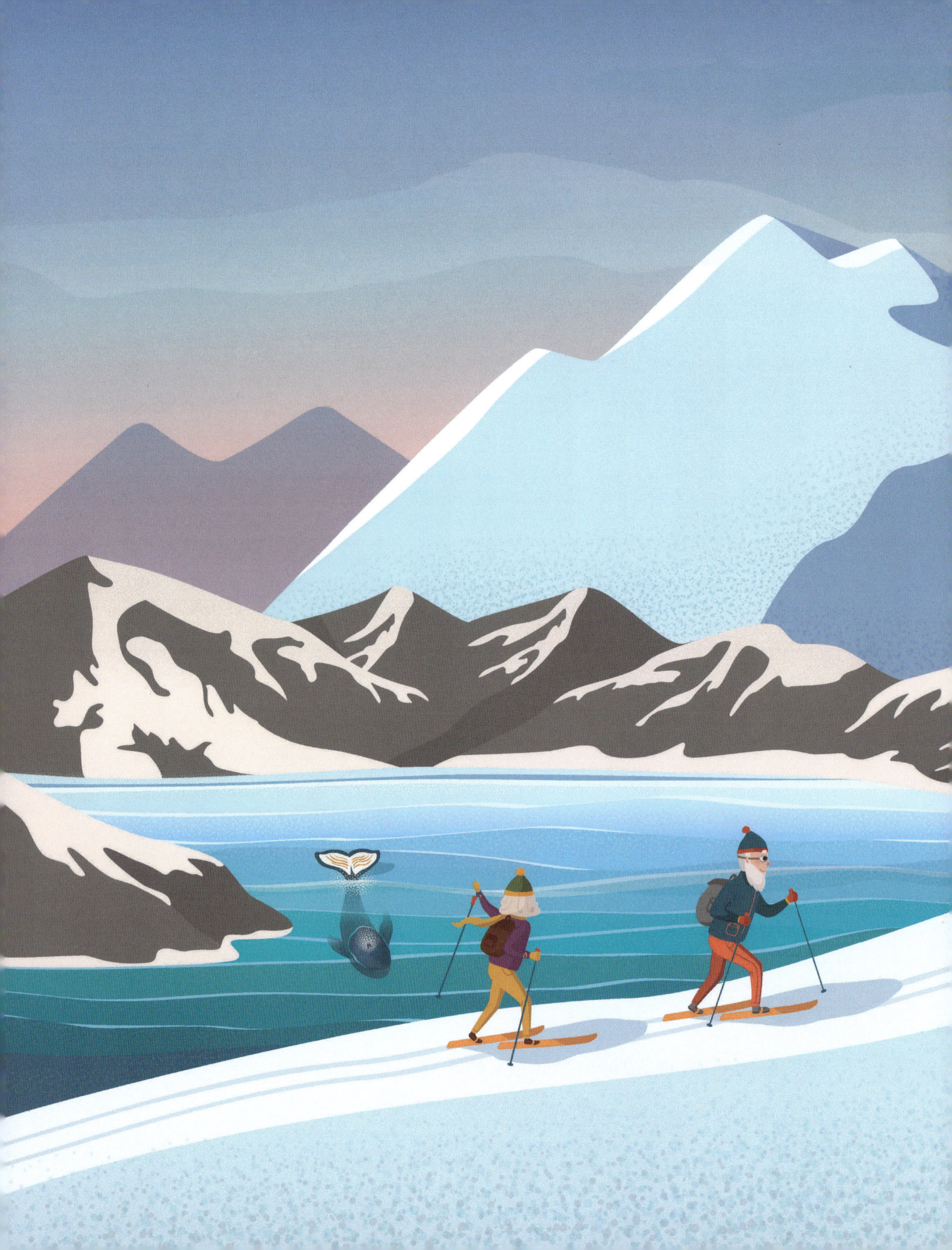

We decided to go skiing with the daddy bear and baby bears along the secret route on the old map. "Look! Musk-oxen and whales!" cried baby bears.

Grandma and I happily continued our kayak trip, and then we saw a penguin!

"Hello, I'm a tourist from Antarctica, floating to see my Arctic friends," said the penguin. And so we made another friend.

We continued our trip, and a large whale emerged from under the water near us.

Grandma patted him, and he disappeared into the deep. "Diving!" exclaimed Grandma.

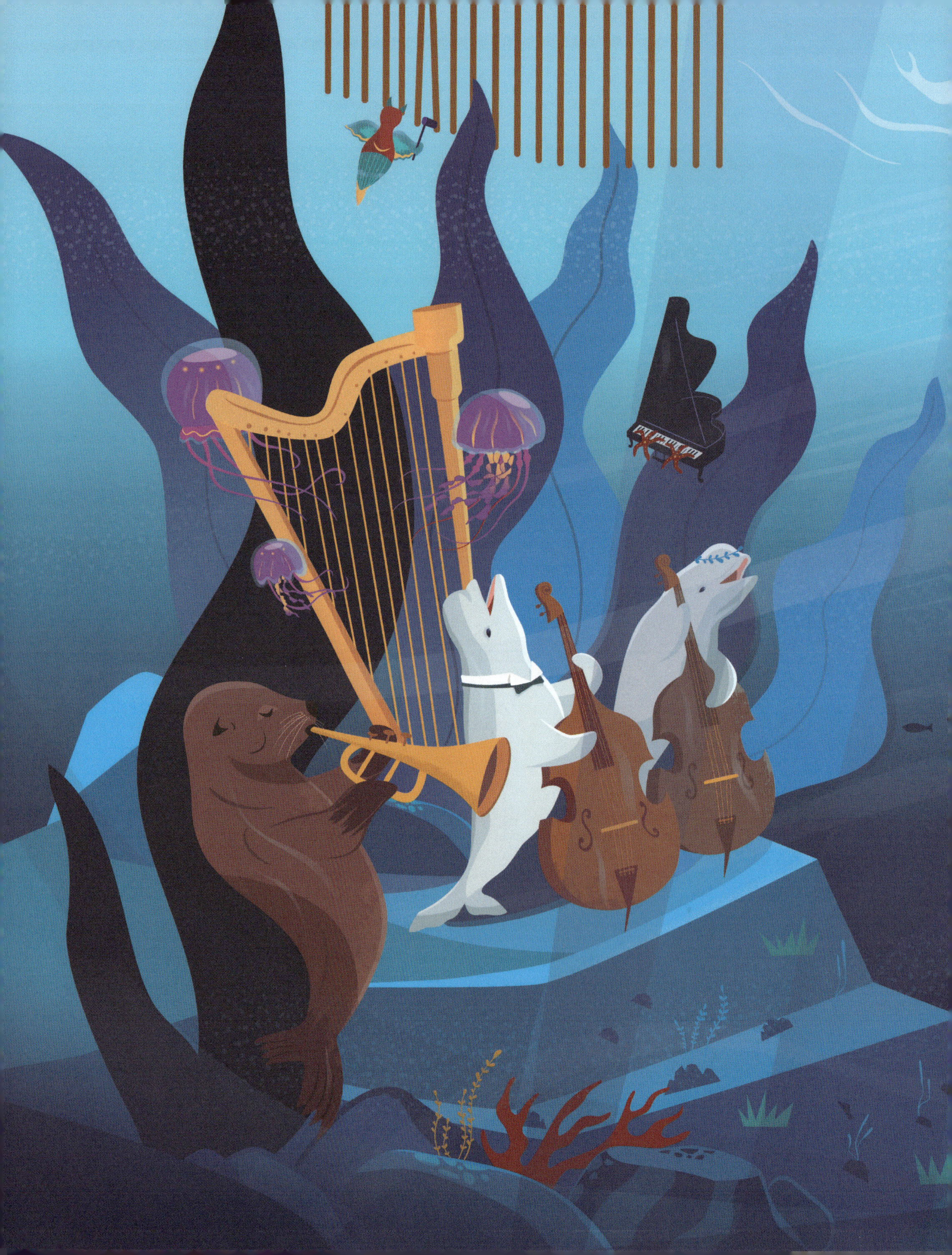

"Wow! The underwater world of the Arctic is fantastic: seals, belugas, narwhals, jellyfish, sea angels..." I thought to myself. The orchestra was playing, and we were quietly enjoying it.

And then we watched the Arctic birds. "Look, the egg is hatching! King Ayder is expecting babies," I said.

"And there, a happy family is looking after their baby," said Grandma. I looked at the old map. We completed our route.

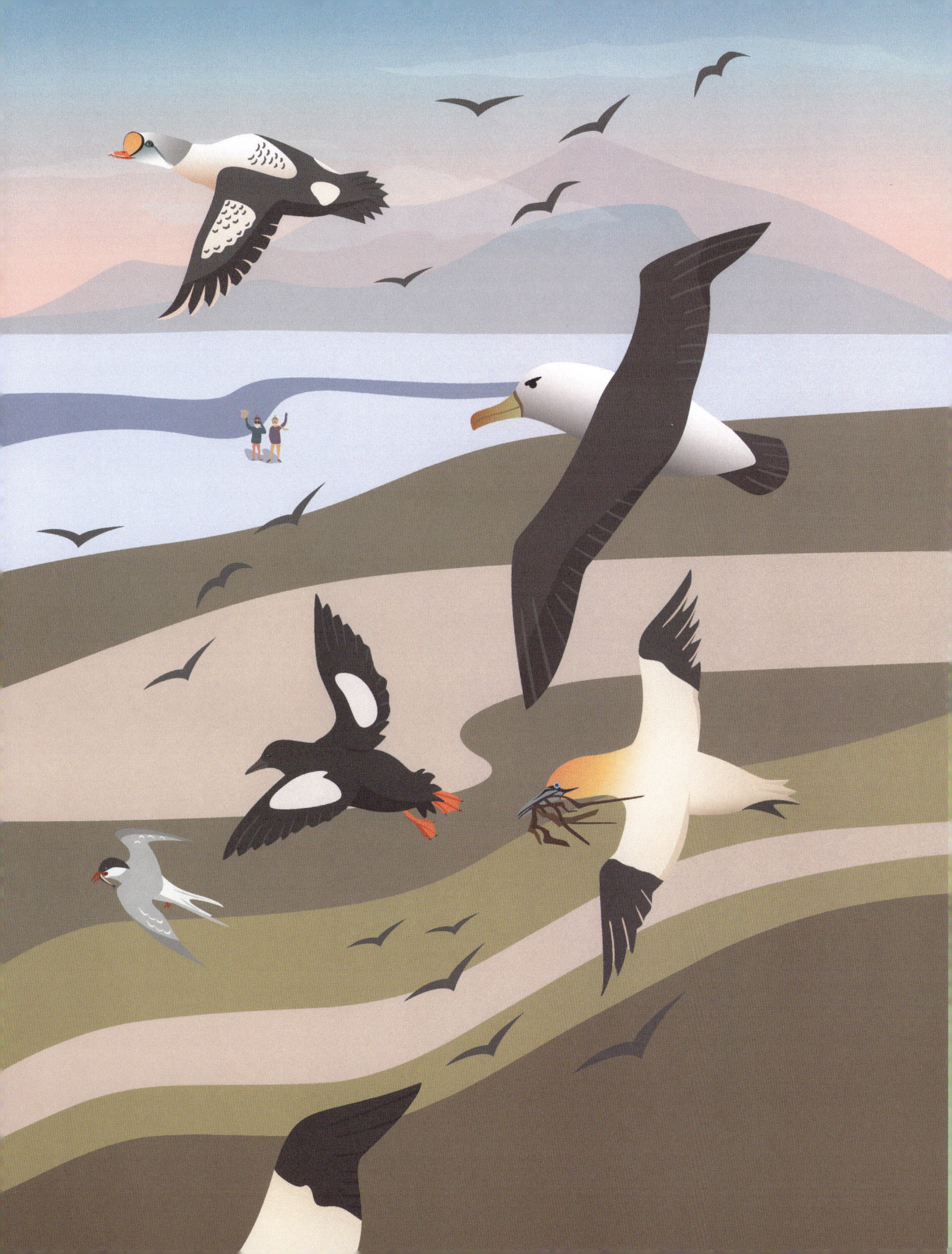

Grandma and I were pleased with our Arctic adventures. We loved our friends so much, and they are saying hello to you. But it's time to go home, our dear friend.

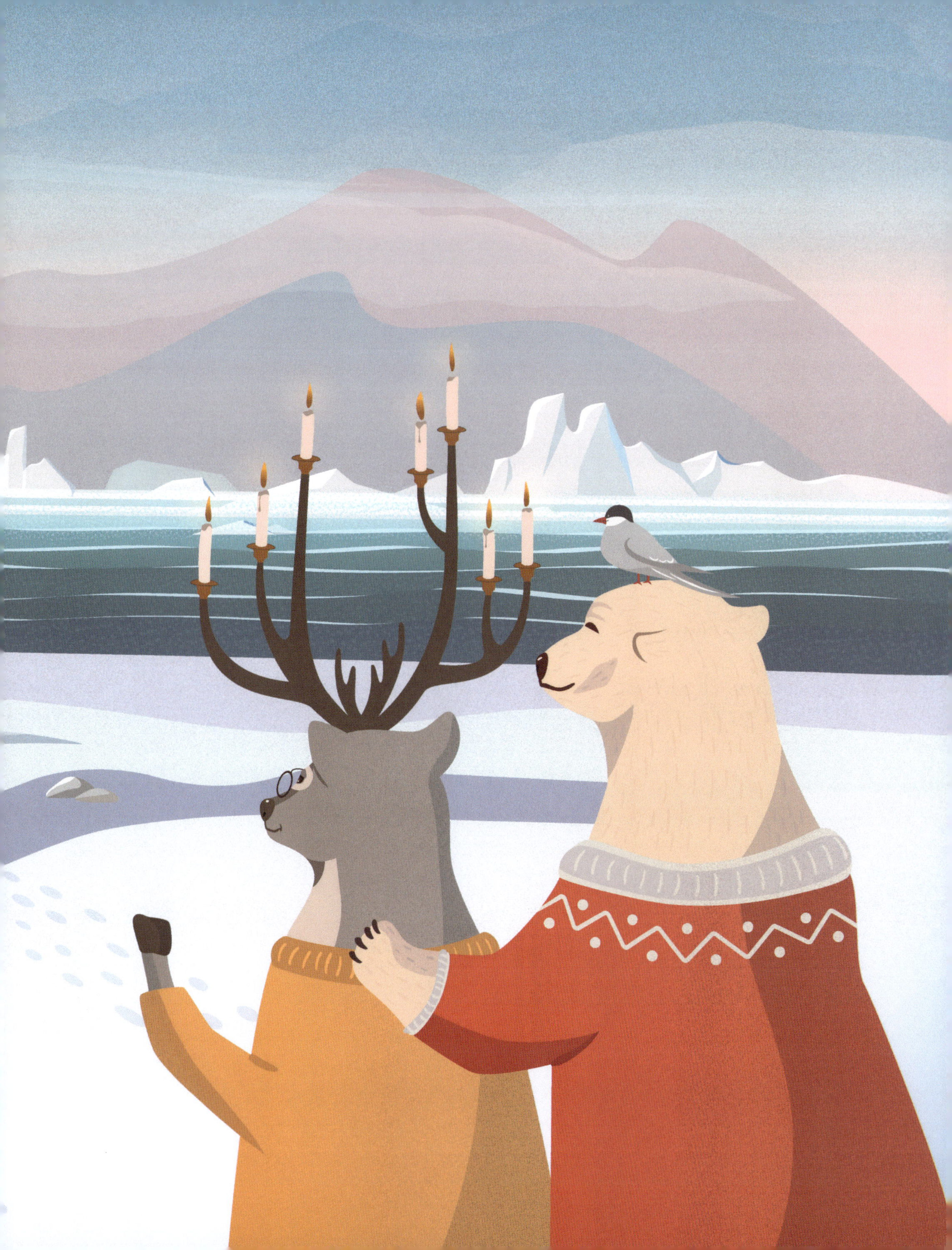

ARCTIC

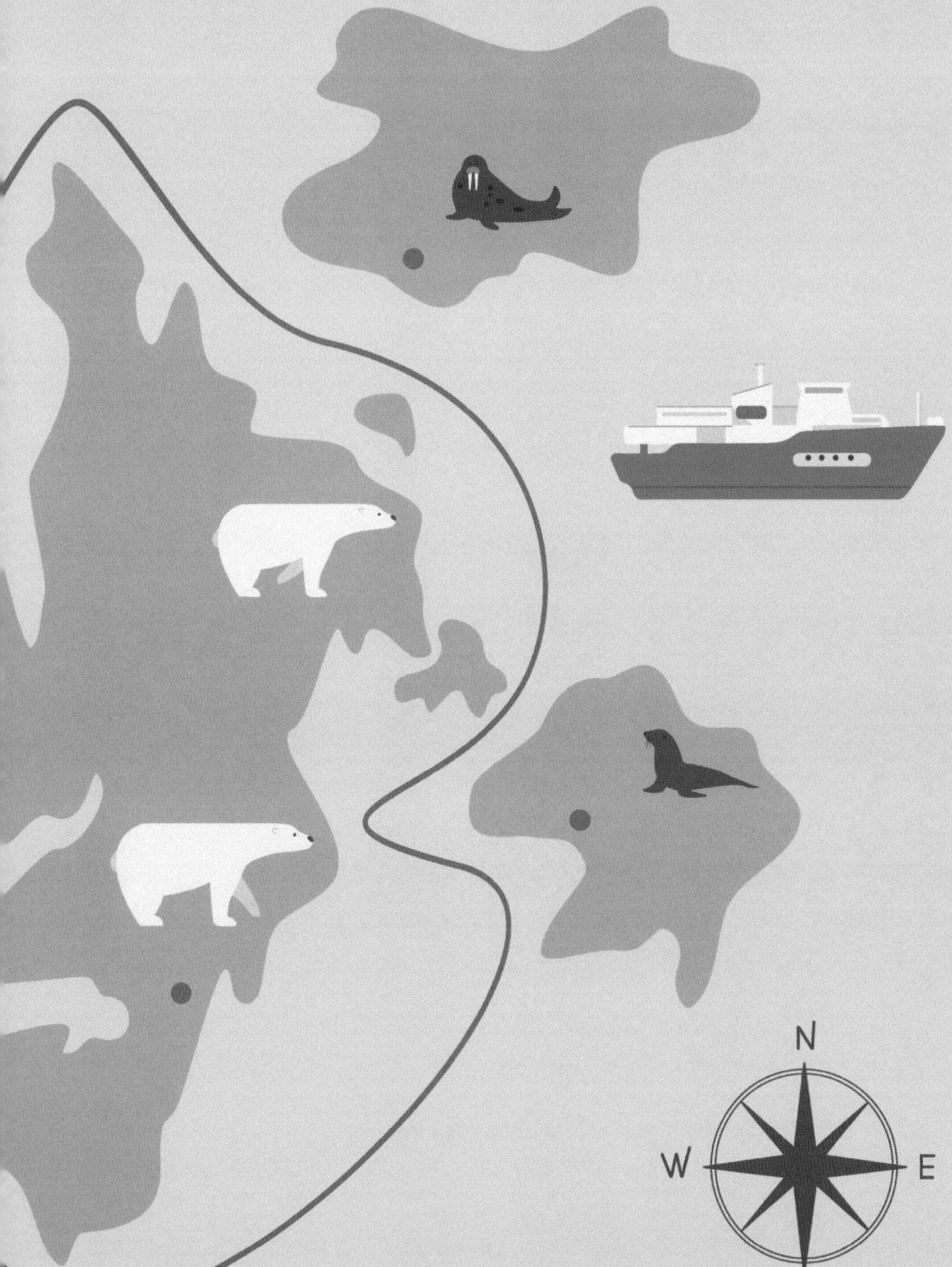
N
W
E
S

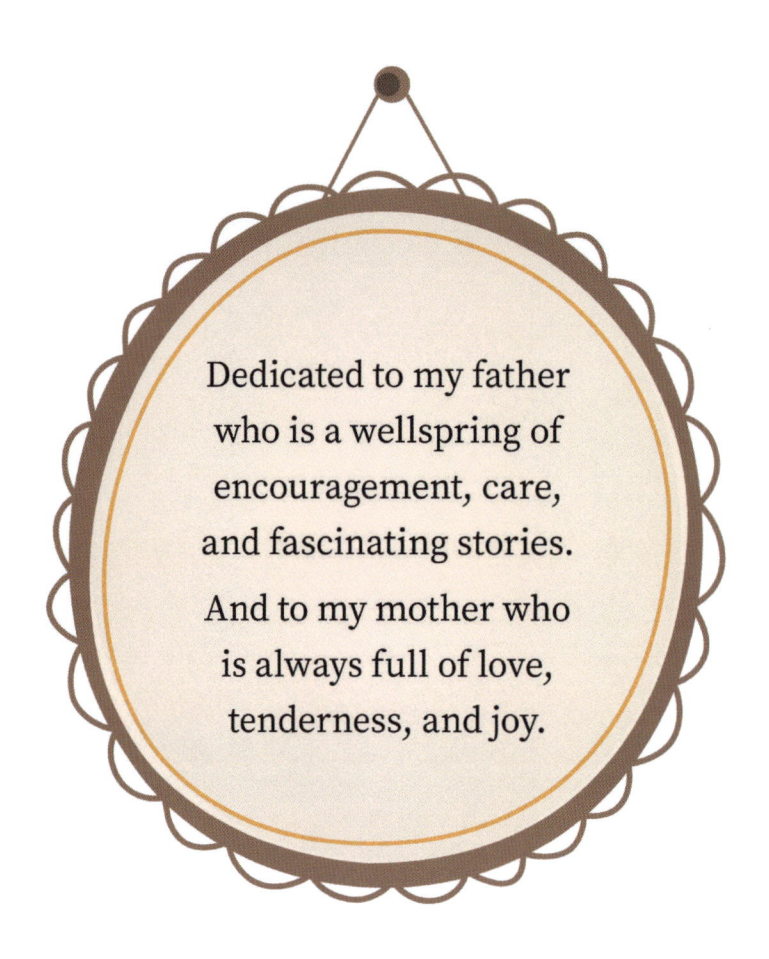

Dedicated to my father who is a wellspring of encouragement, care, and fascinating stories.

And to my mother who is always full of love, tenderness, and joy.

All rights reserved. No part of this publication may be reproduced, stored in a retrieval system, or transmitted, in any form or by any means (electronic, photocopying, mechanical, recording or otherwise), without the prior written permission of the publisher.

Printed in Great Britain
by Amazon